101 Things®
To Do With
Peanut Butter

101 Things To Do With Peanut Butter

BY
PAMELA BENNETT

GIBBS SMITH
TO ENRICH AND INSPIRE HUMANKIND

First Edition
17 16 15   5 4 3 2

Published by
Gibbs Smith
P.O. Box 667
Layton, Utah 84041

1.800.835.4993 orders
www.gibbs-smith.com

Printed and bound in Korea

Gibbs Smith books are printed on either recycled, 100% post-consumer
waste, FSC-certified papers or on paper produced from sustainable PEFC-
certified forest/controlled wood source. Learn more at www.pefc.org.

Library of Congress Cataloging-in-Publication Data

Bennett, Pamela.
  101 things to do with peanut butter / Pamela Bennett. — First edition.
     pages cm
   title: Hundred and one things to do with peanut butter
   title: One hundred and one things to do with peanut butter
   title: One hundred one things to do with peanut butter
   ISBN 978-1-4236-3176-7
1. Cooking (Peanut butter) 2. Cookbooks. lcgft I. Title. II.
Title: Hundred and one things to do with peanut butter. III.
Title: One hundred and one things to do with peanut butter. IV.
Title: One hundred one things to do with peanut butter.
  TX814.5.P38B45 2013
  641.3'56596—dc23
                              2012038334

To Dee. Star and audience. Perfect in both roles.

Yum!
More recipes and tips
at 101yum.com

CONTENTS

Helpful Hints 9

Appetizers

Dips & Sauces

Breakfast, Lunch, & Dinner

Soups, Salads, & Sides

Peanut Butter and Jelly Soup 64 • African Peanut Soup American Style 65 • Peanut and Apple Soup 66 • Jelled Strawberry and Peanut Salad 67 • Confetti Freezer Salad 68 • Zesty Shrimp Salad 69 • Paradise Peanut Slaw 70 • Zippy Potato Salad 71 • Southern Sweet Potatoes 72 • Peanut Butter Potato Cakes 73 • Peanut Butter Biscuits 74

Vegan Lovers

Vegan "Salmon" Party Spread 76 • Roasted Peanut and Garlic Aioli 77 • Breakfast Scramble 78 • Crunchy Eggplant 79 • Peanut Butter Pumpkin Soup 80 • Vegan Gumbo 81 • Chowda 82 • Barbecued Tofu 83 • Mother Earth's Meatloaf 84 • Vegan Peanut Butter Bars 85 • Alien Bites 86 • Faux Moo Pie 87

Sweet Treats

Perfect Peanut Butter Frosting 90 • No Stir-Crazy Cookie Bars 91 • Lazy Day Bars 92 • Country Club Bars 93 • Blondies 94 • Peanut Butter and Jelly Bars 95 • Peanut Butter Cookies 96 • Flat Tires 97 • Peanut Butter Cake Balls 98 • Peanut Butter Party Cups 99 • Movie Night Grab Bag 100 • Peanut Butter and Chocolate Eggs 101 • Needle-in-a-Haystack 102 • Porcupines 103 • Peanut Butter Sesame Drops 104 • Little Darlin's Trail Mix 105

Desserts

Memphis Decadence 108 • Peanut Butter Bread Pudding 109 • Peanut Butter Flan 110 • Dessert Pizza 111 • Pear and Peanut Butter Crisp 112 • Peanut Butter Trifle 113 • Peanut Butter and Banana Cream Pie 114 • Easy as Pie 115 • Birthday Party Pie 116 • Heath Bar Pie 117 • Queen of Hearts Dessert 118 • Stuffed Apples 119 • Peanut Butter Cheesecake 120 • Peanut Butter Pound Cake 121 • Peanut Butter and Apple Enchiladas 122

HELPFUL HINTS

I. When a child gets gum stuck in his/her hair, rub a spoonful of peanut butter all around the gum and hair. The gum will slide out without much tugging, pulling, or tears.

2. Peanut butter is a wonderful substitute for butter when baking cakes or cookies. The consistency remains the same, but with a subtle nuttier taste. When used in lieu of butter to make fudge brownies, the results taste like a delicious, enormous peanut butter cup.

3. A small dab of peanut butter applied with a clean white cloth will aid in removing stains from leather furniture. Buff in a circular motion. (This tip is best for small surface stains.)

4. Those annoying price tags/stickers that refuse to budge when you get that new item home can easily be removed by applying peanut butter to the tag and rubbing off with a sponge.

5. Gum or other gooey messes stuck in your carpet? Dab peanut butter around the perimeter of the gum and remove with a paper towel or cloth.

6. Pet lovers rejoice when it's time to give your dog medicine! Wrap the pill around a small ball of peanut butter. Although dogs have a keen sense of smell to detect medicine, they'll eat the peanut butter treat you offer, by spoon or your hand. They love it! (Low-fat peanut butter would be recommended for pets on a diet.)

7. Peanut butter is an outstanding lubricant for yard tools. If your lawn mower is the push type, smear on some peanut butter to oil the blades. It also works well on dull hedge clippers and other yard tools. Wipe on, and then remove.

8. We love cooking and eating fish at our house but we don't like the fishy smell. After cooking, remove fish from the pan, add 2–3 tablespoons of peanut butter, and cook for about 2 minutes. The aroma of fish disappears.

9. Mice, like humans, enjoy peanut butter. As a matter of fact, peanut butter is one of their favorite treats. So, if you are being visited by a rodent pest, set the trap with peanut butter, and you'll be rid of this problem.

10. One of the greatest innovations to peanut butter I've recently discovered is powdered peanut butter. It comes in re-sealable packages for easy transport when you're on a camping trip, working out at the gym, or any occasion where storage is a premium. Available options are gluten-free, contain 70 percent fewer calories, and 90 percent less fat, and include regular, chunky, raspberry-flavored, chocolate, and sugar-free. The powdered versions of peanut butter are excellent when making shakes and smoothies, toppings for desserts, or any favorite recipe.

11. Two excellent online sources for powdered peanut butter are fitnutzbutter.com and bellplantation.com. These products will revolutionize your peanut butter world!

12. Flavored peanut butter can be found in local specialty shops and online. Popular brands include Peanut Butter & Company, and Nutty's Old Fashioned Peanut Butter.

APPETIZERS

PARTY PEANUT CHICKEN HORS D'OEUVRES

I pound	**ground chicken**
4 tablespoons	**crunchy peanut butter**
2	**green onions,** chopped
I teaspoon	**grated fresh ginger**
I	**garlic clove,** peeled and chopped
2–3 tablespoons	**chili sauce**
I tablespoon	**soy sauce**
¾ cup	**breadcrumbs**
¼ cup	**chopped fresh cilantro or parsley**

Preheat oven to 350 degrees.

Combine all ingredients in a medium bowl and mix well. Roll into 1-inch balls. Place in an 8 x 8-inch glass dish, and bake uncovered for 20–25 minutes, or until juices run clear. Makes 24.

Serve with toothpicks and Traditional Peanut Satay Sauce on page 28.

CHEESY PEANUT BUTTER BALL

1 package (8 ounces)	**cream cheese,** softened
1 cup	**powdered sugar**
3–4 tablespoons	**sugar**
¾ cup	**crunchy peanut butter**
1 package (9 ounces)	**peanut butter chips**

In a medium bowl, beat the cream cheese, sugars, and peanut butter with a hand mixer until well blended. Spoon onto a large piece of plastic wrap, pull up all 4 corners, and twist into shape of a ball. Wrap with more plastic wrap and place in freezer for 1 ½ hours.

Remove from freezer, uncover, and roll in peanut butter chips to cover, pressing to make sure chips adhere. Cover and freeze 2 more hours. Let stand at room temperature for about 15 minutes before serving. Makes 2 cups.

Serve with crackers, small party biscuits, or fresh fruits.

PARTY POPPERS

1/3 cup	**peanut butter**
3 tablespoons	**butter or margarine,** softened
3 tablespoons	**corn syrup**
1 tablespoon	**orange zest**
1 tablespoon	**vanilla extract**
1/2 teaspoon	**salt**
2 cups	**powdered sugar**
1 pound	**pecan or walnut halves**
3 pounds	**large pitted dates**

In a large mixing bowl, cream the peanut butter and butter together with a hand mixer. Add the corn syrup, zest, vanilla, and salt. Mix well. Stir in all of the powdered sugar. After blending completely, move mixture to a board on your countertop that has been sprinkled with additional powdered sugar to help prevent sticking, and knead until all ingredients are thoroughly combined. Wrap in aluminum foil or plastic wrap and refrigerate for at least 4 hours, or overnight.

Remove mixture from refrigerator. Cover each pecan half with 1/2–1 teaspoon of mixture and stuff 1 coated nut into each date. Makes 48.

FIRE ANTS ON A LOG

	hot sauce of choice, to taste
$^1/_2$ cup	**peanut butter**
I	**medium jalapeno***
6–8 stalks	**celery**
$^1/_4$ cup	**chopped raisins or dates**

In a small bowl, mix together hot sauce and peanut butter. Chop the jalapeno to a fine mince and add to peanut butter. Avoid touching eyes or mouth. If you prefer you can use plastic gloves.

Spread peanut butter onto clean, dried stalks of celery. Top with raisins and cut celery into bite-sized pieces. Makes 36–48 Bites.

*Note: You can control the heat by leaving out the seeds, or only using a small amount.

PEANUT BUTTER WINGS

2 1/2 pounds	**chicken wings**
1/3 cup	**peanut butter**
2 teaspoons	**curry powder**
4 tablespoons	**lemon juice**
1 tablespoon	**brown sugar**
3 tablespoons	**soy sauce**
2 tablespoons	**ground ginger**
3	**garlic cloves,** peeled and minced
1 tablespoon	**peanut oil**
1 teaspoon	**Tabasco Sauce**
dash	**salt and pepper**

Cut and trim chicken wing tips; separate into 2 pieces at the joint.

Mix remaining ingredients together in a small bowl. Place marinade and chicken in a large ziplock bag and marinate for 1 1/2 hours in the refrigerator. Take out 1/2 hour before grilling. Remove wings from bag, reserving marinade.

Grill or broil wings until browned and cooked through, about 15–20 minutes, turning over after the first 10 minutes. Baste with marinade while grilling. Makes 3–4 servings.

PEANUT BUTTER WONTONS

24	**wonton wrappers**
1 package (12 ounces)	**white chocolate chips**
1 jar (12 ounces)	**peanut butter**
1/3 cup	**peanut oil**

Place 6 or more chocolate chips on each wonton wrapper. Spoon peanut butter into a large ziplock bag. Cut off a small corner of the bag and drizzle an ample amount of peanut butter over top of chocolate chips. Lightly wet edges of the wrappers with water and fold wrapper into a triangle shape, sealing edges.

Preheat oil in a large frying pan, and fry wontons until crispy on medium-high heat for 2–3 minutes. Remove and let drain on a paper towel. Makes 24.

PB LITTLE SMOKIES

1 package (16 ounces)	**little smokie sausages**
2/3 cup	**cherry or blackberry jam**
1/2 cup	**barbecue sauce**
2 tablespoons	**lemon juice**
1/4 cup	**peanut butter**
1/4 cup	**beef broth**

Heat sausages in a medium frying pan as directed on package.

Mix jam and barbecue sauce in a small saucepan, cooking over medium heat until well blended. Stir in lemon juice and cook for 1 minute. Remove from heat. Add the peanut butter and mix well. Stir in broth, return to heat, and bring to a boil. Remove from heat as soon as boil is reached.

Place all ingredients in a 2-quart slow cooker on low heat to serve. If sauce is too thick for your preference, add water, in increments to desired consistency. Makes 4–6 servings.

LETTUCE WRAPS

6 tablespoons	**crunchy peanut butter**
3–4 tablespoons	**hoisin sauce**
1/2 teaspoon	**vinegar**
1/2 package (6 ounces)	**Thai or Vietnamese glass noodles**
1 cup	**grated carrots**
1 cup	**julienned red bell pepper**
1 cup	**diced fresh mushrooms**
1/4 cup	**chopped peanuts**
1 teaspoon	**red pepper flakes**
1 head	**Boston or Bibb lettuce**
1 cup	**broccoli or alfalfa sprouts**

In a small bowl, whisk peanut butter, hoisin, and vinegar together, blending until smooth.

In a medium saucepan, cook noodles in boiling water for 2 minutes. Remove to a colander and rinse in cold water. Drain.

In a large bowl, mix together the noodles, carrots, bell pepper, mushrooms, peanuts, and pepper flakes. Pour in half of the peanut sauce and toss to coat. Divide mixture and roll up inside the lettuce leaves, tucking in sprouts as the top layer. Serve with remaining peanut sauce. Makes 4 servings.

EMPANADAS

1 pound	**beef stew meat,** diced
1 can (12 ounces)	**cola**
1/3 cup	**chopped onion**
1/2 cup	**chopped green bell pepper**
1	**medium orange, juice and zest**
1/8 cup	**teriyaki sauce**
1/2 cup	**peanut butter**
1 (9-inch)	**refrigerated pie crust,** at room temperature

Preheat oven to 400 degrees.

Place meat in a medium bowl and add the cola. Marinate in refrigerator for 1 hour, discarding cola before cooking the meat. In a medium frying pan over medium-high heat, saute the meat, onion, and bell pepper until onion is translucent and meat is browned and cooked through, about 6–7 minutes.

In a small bowl combine the zest, juice, teriyaki sauce, and peanut butter. Stir until well blended, add to beef mixture, and continue cooking for 2 minutes. Remove from heat and set aside.

Roll out pie crust onto a floured surface to a 16-inch circle. Cut 12 circles of dough using a 3-inch cookie cutter. You may need to re-roll the dough in order to get 12. Lightly brush dough edges with water. Place 1 heaping spoonful of meat mixture onto each dough round. Fold dough over the filling and press edges together with a fork to seal. Place on a baking sheet that has been prepared with nonstick cooking spray and bake for 15 minutes, or until crust starts to turn golden brown. Makes 12.

PEANUT CHICKEN PUFFS

2 cups	**diced boneless, skinless chicken breast**
2 teaspoons	**olive oil**
1/2 cup	**peanut butter**
1 tablespoon	**ground ginger**
1 tablespoon	**lemon juice**
1/8 cup	**milk**
1 tablespoon	**agave nectar or honey**
1 can (8 ounces)	**crescent dinner rolls**
4 tablespoons	**chopped peanuts**
1/2 cup	**chopped fresh basil or cilantro**

Preheat oven to 375 degrees.

In a medium frying pan, cook chicken in oil on medium-high heat until chicken is no longer pink, about 5–6 minutes. Remove chicken from pan and drain on paper towels.

In a small bowl, mix together peanut butter, ginger, lemon juice, milk, and agave until well blended. Set aside.

Unroll crescent rolls, separate, and divide the chicken onto each portion of dough. Roll dough over chicken, brush tops with additional olive oil, and roll in peanuts to cover.

Place on a baking sheet that has been prepared with nonstick cooking spray and bake for 10 minutes, or until golden brown. Sprinkle basil over top and serve with peanut sauce. Makes 8.

TURKEY MEATBALLS IN PEANUT SAUCE

I pound	**ground turkey**
$^1/_2$	**small green or red bell pepper,** seeded and chopped
$^1/_8$ cup	**chopped onion**
$^1/_2$ cup	**panko breadcrumbs**
I teaspoon	**garlic powder**
I	**egg**
2 tablespoons	**olive oil**
I cup	**Bow-Thai Peanut Sauce (page 27)**

Preheat oven to 350 degrees.

In a medium bowl, add turkey, bell pepper, onion, breadcrumbs, garlic, and egg. Mix well to combine and roll into 1-inch balls.

In a large frying pan, saute meatballs in oil over medium-high heat until browned; do not overcook. Drain meatballs and place in a 2-quart casserole dish. Pour peanut sauce over top and bake covered for 20–25 minutes. Makes 4 servings.

SPICY SCALLOPS

I pound	**large scallops**
¼ cup	**crunchy peanut butter**
2 tablespoons	**lemon juice**
I tablespoon	**lemon pepper**
I teaspoon	**creamed horseradish**
I teaspoon	**red pepper flakes**
	salt and pepper, to taste
3 tablespoons	**water**
3 tablespoons	**butter or margarine**
I teaspoon	**parsley flakes**

Place scallops in colander and rinse in cold water. Pat dry and set aside.

In a small bowl, combine peanut butter, lemon juice, lemon pepper, horseradish, pepper flakes, salt, and pepper. Mix well and set aside. Use water if needed to thin sauce if too thick.

In a large frying pan over medium-high heat, saute scallops in butter for 5–7 minutes. Add sauce to scallops and cook for I minute. Remove from heat and garnish with parsley. Makes 3–4 servings.

DIPS & SAUCES

HOMEMADE PEANUT BUTTER

2 cups	**shelled, roasted, unsalted peanuts**
1 tablespoon	**peanut oil**
1/2 teaspoon	**salt**

Place all the ingredients in a food processor and blend for 3 minutes. A ball will form but will eventually disappear as you continue to process. You may need to stop and scrape the blade once or twice. Resume processing until you've reached desired consistency. Keep refrigerated. Makes 1 cup.

BOW-THAI PEANUT SAUCE

2	**garlic cloves,** peeled and finely minced
4 tablespoons	**sesame oil**
$^1/_2$ cup	**peanut butter**
I teaspoon	**curry powder**
$^1/_4$ cup	**coconut milk**
4 tablespoons	**lemon juice**
2 tablespoons	**brown sugar**
I teaspoon	**cinnamon**

In a small saucepan, saute garlic in oil for about 3 minutes. Add remaining ingredients, stirring well. Bring to a boil, reduce heat, and simmer 2–3 minutes until sauce is well incorporated. Serve when cool. Makes I cup.

Delicious with spring rolls, chicken skewers, fried rice, stuffed lettuce cups, and Thai main dishes.

TRADITIONAL PEANUT SATAY SAUCE

1	**lime,** juice and zest
1/2 cup	**crunchy peanut butter**
1	**small red chile,** seeded
	and chopped
1/4 cup	**coconut milk**
	salt, to taste
	sugar, to taste

Squeeze the lime juice into a blender, add zest and remaining ingredients; pulse for 15–20 seconds. Adjust coconut milk for desired consistency. Makes 3/4 cup.

Serve at room temperature with curries, Asian noodle dishes, or as a dip for spring rolls, egg rolls, and tempura.

LUSCIOUS AUTUMN DIP

³/₄ cup	**peanut butter**
³/₄ cup	**canned pumpkin**
¹/₂ cup	**brown sugar**
1 tablespoon	**vanilla extract**
1 teaspoon	**nutmeg**
1 teaspoon	**cinnamon**

Combine all ingredients in a medium microwave safe bowl and heat in microwave for 2 minutes. Stir thoroughly to combine. Makes 1 ¹/₂ cups.

Serve with pears, apples, carrots, ice cream, or nut and fruit breads. Refrigerate any leftovers.

GOOD KARMA SAUCE

³/4 cup	**peanut butter**
I cup	**plain yogurt**
2 tablespoons	**tikka or garam masala**
¹/4 cup	**golden raisins**
2 tablespoons	**brown sugar**
2	**garlic cloves,** peeled
2 tablespoons	**grated fresh ginger**
2 teaspoons	**Sriracha hot sauce**
I tablespoon	**lemon juice**
	salt, to taste

Combine all ingredients in a blender or food processor and pulse for I minute. Refrigerate and serve cold. Makes I ³/4 cups.

Serve with naan, or other Indian dishes.

FISH TACO SAUCE

³/₄ cup	**peanut butter**
¹/₄ cup	**hot water**
¹/₄ cup	**honey**
4 teaspoons	**soy sauce**
2 teaspoons	**grated fresh ginger**

Combine all ingredients in a small bowl. Stir until well blended. Serve at room temperature. Makes 1 cup.

This is a great marinade for grilling fish or shrimp, and excellent as a dip for pot stickers, Asian dumplings, or spring rolls.

PEANUT COLADA DIP

¹/₃ cup	**peanut butter**
³/₄ cup	**coconut milk**
I can (8 ounces)	**crushed pineapple,** with juice
¹/₂ cup	**sour cream**
I small box (3.4 ounces)	**instant coconut pudding mix**

Combine all ingredients in a medium bowl and mix until well blended. Refrigerate until ready to serve. Makes 2 cups.

Serve with choice of fruit, or over rice.

OOEY-GOOEY DIP

¹/₂ cup	**peanut butter**
¹/₂ cup	**butter or margarine**
¹/₂ cup	**corn syrup**
1 cup	**brown sugar**
1 can (14 ounces)	**sweetened condensed milk**

Place all ingredients in a medium saucepan and stir over low heat until sugar has dissolved. Makes 3 ¹/₂ cups.

Serve in a 1–2 quart slow cooker on low heat with fresh fruit of choice, cheese cubes, or cake bites. Refrigerate any leftovers.

PEANUT BUTTER FONDUE

1 cup	**peanut butter**
1/4 cup	**milk**
1 teaspoon	**butter or margarine**
2 tablespoons	**brown sugar**
1/2 cup	**chocolate syrup**
1/2 teaspoon	**salt**

Combine all ingredients in a medium saucepan and stir over low heat until sugar has dissolved. Makes 1 3/4 cups.

Serve in a 1–2 quart slow cooker on low heat, or a fondue pot with fresh fruit of choice, cake bites, marshmallows, or over ice cream. Refrigerate any leftovers.

PEANUT PESTO

1 1/2 cups	**fresh basil**
1/2 cup	**grated Parmesan cheese**
3 tablespoons	**crunchy peanut butter**
2	**garlic cloves,** peeled
1/3 cup	**olive oil**

Place all ingredients in a blender or food processor and blend to desired consistency. Keep in refrigerator for up to 1 week. Makes 1 cup.

Serve on warm or cold pasta, or spread on crusty breads.

PEANUT BUTTER HUMMUS

I can (29 ounces)	**garbanzo beans,** drained and rinsed
3	**garlic cloves,** peeled and minced
1/4 cup	**peanut butter**
3–4 tablespoons	**lemon juice**
1/4 cup	**vegetable broth**
I tablespoon	**olive oil**
1/2 teaspoon	**ground cumin,** or to taste
	salt and pepper, to taste

Place beans, garlic, peanut butter, lemon juice, broth, and oil in a blender. Puree until smooth. Add the cumin, salt, and pepper. If too thick, add a little more oil to desired consistency.

Place in a serving bowl and cover with plastic wrap. Leave on countertop at room temperature for at least I hour before serving. Refrigerate any leftovers. Makes 2 cups.

BREAKFAST, LUNCH, & DINNER

PEANUT BUTTER CREPES

Crepes:

1 1/2 cups	**flour**
3	**eggs**
1 1/4 cups	**milk**
2 tablespoons	**butter or margarine,** melted
4 tablespoons	**peanut butter**
dash	**salt**

Filling:

1/3 cup	**peanut butter**
1/3 cup	**Nutella spread**
2	**bananas,** peeled and sliced
1 can (7 or 14 ounces)	**Redi-Whip**

Place crepe ingredients in a blender and blend for 1 minute on medium speed. Let batter stand at room temperature at least 1 hour before cooking.

Preheat a 10-inch crepe pan or frying pan that has been prepared with nonstick cooking spray. Pour 1/4 cup of batter in hot pan. Immediately tilt the pan to evenly coat the bottom of the pan with batter. Return to the burner. Cook for 30–60 seconds, or until top appears dry. Flip crepe and cook an additional 30 seconds. Continue with remaining batter.

Divide peanut butter and Nutella into equal portions and spread over each crepe. Top with banana slices and Redi-Whip; roll up. Makes 4 servings.

PEANUT BUTTER MUFFINS

2 cups	**flour**
$\frac{1}{2}$ cup	**sugar**
2 $\frac{1}{2}$ teaspoons	**baking powder**
$\frac{1}{2}$ teaspoon	**salt**
$\frac{1}{2}$ cup	**peanut butter**
2 tablespoons	**butter or margarine**
I cup	**milk**
2	**eggs**

Preheat oven to 400 degrees.

Prepare muffin tin with nonstick cooking spray or cupcake liners.

In a large bowl, sift together the flour, sugar, baking powder, and salt. Cut the peanut butter and butter into the flour using a pastry cutter or 2 forks, until you get pea-sized crumbles. Add the milk and eggs and beat on medium speed with a hand mixer until well combined. Batter will be slightly thick.

Fill muffin cups $\frac{2}{3}$ full and bake for I5 minutes, or until center springs back to the touch. Makes I2.

PEANUT BUTTER OMELET

3	**eggs or $3/4$ cup egg substitute**
pinch	**salt**
pinch	**sugar**
1	**banana,** peeled and sliced
2–3 tablespoons	**peanut butter**
$1/3$ cup	**chopped peanuts**

Prepare a medium frying pan with cooking spray and heat on medium–high heat.

In a small bowl, whisk the eggs and pour into the pan. Sprinkle salt and sugar over eggs and top with banana slices. Cook for about 1 minute. Using a spatula, gently lift sides of the omelet so the runny eggs flow underneath. Continue cooking and flip completely over when omelet starts to hold together.

Spread the peanut butter and chopped peanuts over half of the omelet. Fold and continue cooking until no longer runny. Flip over and cook for 1 minute more before serving. Makes 1–2 servings.

BAKED FRENCH TOAST

I teaspoon	**butter or margarine**
I loaf	**cinnamon bread,** cubed
5	**eggs**
2 1/2 cups	**milk**
1/2 cup	**peanut butter**
2 teaspoons	**vanilla extract**

Preheat oven to 350 degrees.

Grease the bottom and sides of a 9 x 9-inch baking dish with butter and spread bread cubes evenly over bottom of dish.

Place remaining ingredients in a medium bowl and beat until thoroughly combined. Pour mixture over the bread. Place dish in the refrigerator and let bread soak for at least I hour, or overnight. Bake uncovered for 45–50 minutes. Makes 4 servings.

SATURDAY MORNING TOAST

6 slices	**Texas toast**
1/2 cup	**crunchy peanut butter**
1/2 cup	**orange marmalade**
1/3 cup	**raisins**
1/3 cup	**shredded coconut**
4 tablespoons	**cinnamon**
4 tablespoons	**sugar**

Divide peanut butter between each bread slice and spread evenly over top. Spread marmalade over peanut butter and top with raisins, coconut, cinnamon, and sugar.

Place under broiler for 2 minutes, or until peanut butter starts to melt and edges of bread start to brown. Makes 6 servings.

HOMEMADE POP TARTS

1 (9-inch)	**refrigerated pie crust,** at room temperature
1 jar	**flavored peanut butter***
1 cup	**powdered sugar**
3–4 tablespoons	**milk**
1/3 cup	**sprinkles or colored sugar**

Preheat oven to 350 degrees.

Roll out pie crust to 12 inches and cut dough into 4 evenly shaped rectangles. Place 1 large tablespoon of peanut butter in the center of 2 rectangles and spread, but not to the edges, and cover with another piece of dough. Press edges together with fork, or pinch with fingers. Place on a baking sheet that has been prepared with nonstick cooking spray and bake for 15–20 minutes.

In a small bowl, mix together the sugar and milk until smooth. Spread icing over top of cooled pop tarts and top with sprinkles. Makes 2 servings.

Note: see Helpful Hints #12, page 10.

PEANUT BUTTER PANCAKES

2 cups	**biscuit mix**
1 cup	**milk**
2	**eggs**
1/3 cup	**peanut butter**

Heat an electric griddle to 350 degrees. Prepare griddle with nonstick cooking spray.

Place all ingredients in a blender and blend until smooth. Pour 1/4 cup batter per pancake evenly onto hot griddle. Cook for 1–2 minutes on each side until golden brown. Makes 2–4 servings.

PEANUT BUTTER ROLL-UPS

2 (10-inch)	**flour tortillas**
⅓ cup	**peanut butter**
1	**banana,** peeled and sliced
4–6	**large strawberries,** hulled and sliced
3 tablespoons	**shredded coconut**
2–3 teaspoons	**crushed candied pecans** **or almonds**
3–4 tablespoons	**yogurt or sour cream**
½ teaspoon	**brown sugar**

Generously spread one side of each tortilla with peanut butter and top with bananas, strawberries, coconut, and nuts.

In a small bowl, mix together the yogurt and sugar and drizzle over top of tortillas. Roll up tortillas, cut into halves, and secure with toothpicks. Makes 2 servings.

DESERT DELIGHT SANDWICH SPREAD

3/4 cup	**golden raisins**
1/2 cup	**chopped dates**
1/2 cup	**apple juice**
I cup	**peanut butter**
2 tablespoons	**honey**
I teaspoon	**ground ginger**
I teaspoon	**cinnamon**
1/4 cup	**slivered almonds**
2	**large croissants,** sliced in half lengthwise
I	**banana,** peeled and sliced

In a medium saucepan bring raisins, dates, and juice to a low boil; simmer uncovered for 10 minutes. Add peanut butter, honey, ginger, and cinnamon and cook on low heat for 3 minutes. Mixture should be the consistency of a curd or fruity jam. Remove from heat and cool slightly. Add the almonds and mix well.

Top each croissant half with banana slices, and spoon mixture evenly over top. This can be served as-is or finished under the broiler for about 2 minutes, or until bananas start to caramelize. Makes 2 servings.

PUMPKIN PEANUT BUTTER SANDWICH

3 tablespoons	**canned pumpkin puree**
3 tablespoons	**peanut butter**
1 teaspoon	**brown sugar or agave nectar**
4 slices	**banana, cranberry, or zucchini bread**
1	**banana,** peeled and sliced
3–4	**strawberries,** hulled and sliced

In a small bowl mix together pumpkin, peanut butter, and sugar until well combined. Spread generously over bread slices and top with fruit. Serve open-faced. Makes 2 servings.

THAI CHICKEN OR TOFU PIZZA

I cup	**peanut butter**
¼ cup	**coconut milk**
3 tablespoons	**brown sugar**
I tablespoon	**Thai chili sauce or favorite hot sauce**
4 (8-inch)	**pita breads**
6–8	**green onions,** sliced
I ½ cups	**grated carrots**
2 cups	**diced cooked chicken or grilled tofu**
I cup	**chopped fresh basil**
2 cups	**crushed peanuts**
2 cups	**grated mozzarella cheese**

Preheat oven to 400 degrees.

In a small bowl, combine peanut butter, milk, sugar, and chili sauce. Whisk until smooth. If sauce is too thick, add more milk to desired consistency.

Spread peanut sauce generously over each pita and top evenly with remaining ingredients in the order listed. Place pitas on a 10-inch or larger pizza pan and bake for 5–7 minutes, or until cheese has melted. Makes 4 servings.

LUAU WRAP

6	**boneless, skinless chicken breasts**
¹/₂ pound	**bacon,** chopped
¹/₂ cup	**crunchy peanut butter**
1 cup	**teriyaki sauce**
1 can (20 ounces)	**crushed pineapple,** drained
6–8 (10-inch)	**flour tortillas**
¹/₂ cup	**chopped scallions**
¹/₂ cup	**chopped carrots**
¹/₂ cup	**chopped lettuce**

Preheat oven to 375 degrees.

Place chicken breasts between two pieces of plastic wrap and pound with a rolling pin or mallet to flatten. Cut into strips and place in a 9 x 13-inch baking dish. Sprinkle bacon over top.

In a small bowl, mix together the peanut butter and teriyaki sauce until smooth. Add in the pineapple and pour over the chicken and bacon. Allow to marinate for 30 minutes on the countertop or in the refrigerator. Bake covered for 30–40 minutes.

Assemble wraps by placing equal portions of chicken and vegetables on top of tortillas; roll and serve seam side down. Makes 6–8 servings.

HAM ROLL-UPS

I box (6 ounces)	**cornbread stuffing mix**
I can (28 ounces)	**cherry pie filling**
1/2 cup	**peanut butter**
6 tablespoons	**brown sugar**
6 large pieces	**ham,** sliced thin

Preheat oven to 350 degrees.

Prepare stuffing mix according to package directions and set aside.

In a small bowl, combine pie filling, peanut butter, and sugar. Mix well.

Divide the stuffing into equal portions and spoon down the middle of each ham slice. Fold over and secure with toothpicks or kitchen twine. Place in a 9 x 13-inch baking dish that has been prepared with nonstick cooking spray, seam side down, and pour peanut butter mixture over top. Bake covered for 20 minutes, or until sauce is hot and bubbling. Make 6 servings.

CHINESE PATTIES

8	**eggs,** beaten
I cup	**bean sprouts**
I cup	**chopped fresh mushrooms**
6	**green onions,** chopped
¼ cup	**crunchy peanut butter**
I pound	**medium cooked shrimp,** rough chopped
	salt and pepper, to taste
4 tablespoons	**sesame or peanut oil**

In a medium bowl add eggs, sprouts, mushrooms, and onions. Whisk until well blended. Add peanut butter, shrimp, salt, and pepper and stir until thoroughly mixed.

Add oil to a large frying pan and heat to medium-high. Oil will be ready for frying when a drop of water pops up from the pan.

Divide shrimp mixture into 4 equal portions and place in frying pan. Use a spatula to form patties. Cook 4–5 minutes on each side, turning once. Remove cooked patties to a warm plate and cover with paper towels until ready to serve. Makes 4 servings.

Serve with Bow-Thai Peanut Sauce, page 27 or Traditional Peanut Satay Sauce, page 28.

PEANUTTY PASTA

¹/₂ cup	**peanut butter**
¹/₄ cup	**heavy cream**
3 teaspoons	**brown sugar**
3 tablespoons	**lemon juice**
2 tablespoons	**hot sauce**
¹/₂ cup	**grated Parmesan cheese**
I teaspoon	**pepper**
¹/₂ package (16 ounces)	**vermicelli or thin spaghetti**
3	**green onions,** chopped
¹/₄ cup	**chopped peanuts**

In a medium saucepan, add peanut butter, cream, sugar, lemon juice, hot sauce, cheese, and pepper. Stir and cook over medium heat for 5–7 minutes. If sauce is too thick, thin with small increments of water to desired consistency.

In a large saucepan, prepare pasta according to package directions. Drain, but do not rinse. Place pasta in a serving dish and pour sauce over top, tossing to coat. Top with onions and peanuts. Serve hot or cold. Makes 3–4 servings.

GOLDEN CORNISH HENS

2 (1 pound each)	**Cornish game hens**
6 tablespoons	**peanut butter**
4	**green onions,** chopped and divided
4 tablespoons	**soy sauce**
1 teaspoon	**cayenne pepper**
1 teaspoon	**pepper**
2 tablespoons	**vinegar**
2 teaspoons	**ground ginger**
2	**garlic cloves,** peeled and mashed
6 tablespoons	**butter or margarine**

Preheat oven to 350 degrees.

If hens are frozen, defrost according to package directions. Rinse and pat dry.

In a small bowl, combine peanut butter, half of the onions, soy sauce, peppers, and vinegar to make a paste. Gently loosen skin over the breast and leg portions of each hen and rub half of the paste between the skin and meat. Rub any remaining paste over outside skin. Place the remaining onions, ginger, and garlic inside the cavity of the hens.

Place hens in a small roasting pan, adding butter to bottom of the pan. Bake for 1 hour and 20 minutes, or until juices run clear. For a crisp skin, bake uncovered. Makes 2 servings.

THAI SLOW COOKER CHICKEN

6–8	**boneless, skinless chicken breasts**
I bottle (16 ounces)	**Asian salad dressing**
3 tablespoons	**Thai chili paste**
3–4 tablespoons	**grated fresh ginger**
2	**garlic cloves,** peeled and mashed
⅓ cup	**crunchy peanut butter**
3–4	**green onions,** chopped
2 tablespoons	**sugar**

Slice the chicken into strips and place in a 4- to 6-quart slow cooker. In a medium bowl mix together remaining ingredients until well combined. Pour over chicken strips. Cook on low setting 4–5 hours, or until chicken is fork tender. Makes 4–6 servings.

ONE POT GERMAN DINNER

¹/₂ pound	**bacon,** chopped
2 tablespoons	**sugar**
1	**small onion,** peeled and chopped
¹/₂ cup	**peanut butter**
2 tablespoons	**vinegar**
1 cup	**water, broth, or wine**
2	**medium Granny Smith apples,** cored and sliced
4 cups	**chopped red cabbage**
6	**large German sausage links**

In a large frying pan, fry bacon until just crispy. Drain grease reserving 4 tablespoons. In same frying pan, add sugar to the bacon and reserved grease. Cook and stir until sugar turns brown. Add onion and cook until translucent and golden, about 3–4 minutes.

In a small bowl, mix together the peanut butter, vinegar, and choice of liquid until smooth; add to bacon mixture, stirring well to combine.

Assemble ingredients in a 4- to 6-quart slow cooker in the following order: bacon, apples, cabbage, and sausages. Cook on low heat, 3–4 hours, or until sausage is cooked through. Add liquid as needed to prevent sticking. Makes 6 servings.

ISLAND PORK

2 cups	**apple cider**
3/4 cup	**peanut butter**
2 teaspoons	**ground ginger**
3 tablespoons	**sea salt**
1 (4–5 pound)	**boneless pork roast**
1–2 tablespoons	**Liquid Smoke**
1	**small head green cabbage**

Preheat oven to 250 degrees.

In a medium bowl mix together the cider, peanut butter, ginger, and salt until well combined. Place the roast in a small covered roasting pan and pour marinade over top. Spoon Liquid Smoke over the roast.

Remove the largest cabbage leaves and rinse in cold water. Wrap leaves around the pork, covering entire roast. Secure with kitchen string or toothpicks. Place roast in pan and cover with foil or lid. Check roast at 3 hours and every 15 minutes after, until pork is tender and easily shreds with a fork. Makes 6–8 servings.

KARATE CHOPS

4	**thick-cut pork chops**
1 tablespoon	**olive oil**
4 slices	**red onion**
4	**large green bell pepper rings**
1 cup	**plain yogurt or sour cream**
1/4 cup	**peanut butter**
1/4 cup	**milk**
2 tablespoons	**soy sauce**
2 tablespoons	**hot sauce**
1 teaspoon	**thyme or rosemary**
	salt and pepper, to taste
1 tablespoon	**red pepper flakes**

In a large frying pan, saute chops in oil over medium heat until evenly browned, about 5–7 minutes. Drain grease. Top each chop with 1 slice of onion and 1 bell pepper ring.

In a small bowl, combine remaining ingredients and mix well; pour over chops. Cook covered over medium-low heat for 35–45 minutes. Makes 4 servings.

NO PEEHING STEW

2 pounds	**lean beef stew cubes**
4	**large potatoes,** peeled and sliced
2	**small onions,** peeled and sliced
6–8	**carrots,** peeled and sliced
I cup	**sliced celery**
	salt and pepper, to taste
4 tablespoons	**tapioca**
2 cans (11.5 ounces each)	**Snap-E-Tom Tomato & Chile Cocktail**
¹/₂ cup	**peanut butter**
I cup	**water**

Add the meat and vegetables to a 4- to 6-quart slow cooker and season with salt and pepper.

In a medium bowl, dissolve the tapioca in the tomato juice. Add the peanut butter and water and stir until well blended. Pour over the meat and vegetables and cook on low setting for 4–6 hours. Makes 4 servings.

QUICK SHRIMP CURRY

⅓ cup	**butter or margarine**
¼ cup	**chopped onion**
4 tablespoons	**flour**
2 cups	**half-and-half**
⅓ cup	**peanut butter**
4 tablespoons	**curry paste**
1 teaspoon	**saffron,** optional
¼ teaspoon	**paprika**
¼ teaspoon	**nutmeg**
3 tablespoons	**lemon juice**
2 tablespoons	**ground ginger**
1 ½ pounds	**medium shrimp,** peeled and deveined
3 cups	**cooked instant rice**
2 tablespoons	**sambal hot sauce,** or to taste

In a large saucepan, melt the butter and saute onion until translucent. Add flour and half-and-half, stirring constantly so the roux doesn't stick to the pan. Stir in peanut butter, curry, saffron, paprika, nutmeg, lemon juice, and ginger. Cook on low until sauce thickens, about 5 minutes. Add the shrimp and cook until they turn pink; do not overcook. Serve with rice and top with hot sauce. Makes 4–5 servings.

PEANUT CHICKEN OLE

1 cup	**chicken broth**
2 cans (4.5 ounces each)	**chopped green chiles**
2 pounds	**boneless, skinless chicken breasts**
1/4 cup	**olive oil**
1/2 cup	**chopped onion**
1 cup	**milk**
3/4 cup	**crunchy peanut butter**
1/4 cup	**cream cheese**
1 1/3 cups	**grated Monterey Jack cheese,** divided
2 teaspoons	**ground cumin**
1 can (10 ounces)	**enchilada sauce**
12 (6-inch)	**corn tortillas**

Preheat oven to 350 degrees.

Bring chicken broth and 1 can of chiles to boil in a large frying pan. Add the chicken and simmer covered for 15–20 minutes, or until chicken is fully cooked. Remove from heat, cool, and shred, or chop chicken. Reserve remaining broth in a separate bowl and set aside.

In same frying pan add oil, remaining can of chiles, and onion; saute for 3 minutes. Add reserved broth, milk, peanut butter, cream cheese, 1 cup Monterey Jack, cumin, and enchilada sauce. Stir well to blend thoroughly. Add chicken and cook 2–3 minutes.

Place 4 of the tortillas in the bottom of a 2-quart casserole dish that has been prepared with nonstick cooking spray. Spoon 2 cups of chicken mixture over tortillas. Repeat layers. Top with remaining cheese and bake for 30 minutes. Makes 4–6 servings.

CORNBREAD CHILI BAKE

2 cans (15 ounces each)	**hot chili beans**
$^1/_2$	**small onion,** peeled and chopped
$^3/_4$ cup	**grated cheddar cheese**
1 package (8.5 ounces)	**cornbread mix**
$^1/_2$ cup	**crunchy peanut butter**

Pour chili into an 8 x 8-inch baking dish that has been prepared with nonstick cooking spray. Sprinkle onion and cheese over top.

Prepare cornbread according to package directions adding peanut butter to the batter. Mix well. Add more milk if needed so batter will be pourable and not too thick. Pour batter over top of chili and bake for 20 minutes, or until cornbread is cooked through and starts to brown. Makes 4 servings.

SOUPS, SALADS, & SIDES

PEANUT BUTTER AND JELLY SOUP

I can (15 ounces)	**sweet potatoes or yams,** drained
3/4 cup	**peanut butter**
2 cups	**chicken broth**
I cup	**water**
1/4 teaspoon	**garlic powder**
	salt, to taste
1/4 cup	**grape or strawberry jam**

Place sweet potatoes in a blender and puree for 30 seconds, or use a potato masher. Pour puree into a large saucepan, adding remaining ingredients except jam. Cook and stir over medium heat until hot, about 5–6 minutes. Before serving, warm jam in microwave and swirl a small portion into individual soup bowls. Makes 3–4 servings.

AFRICAN PEANUT
SOUP AMERICAN STYLE

I cup	**peanut butter**
5 cubes	**chicken or vegetable bouillon**
4 cups	**water**
I cup	**milk**
$^1/_2$ cup	**sour cream**
I can (I4 ounces)	**diced tomatoes,** with liquid
2	**garlic cloves,** peeled and chopped
3 teaspoons	**curry powder**
I teaspoon	**cayenne pepper**
	salt, to taste
3–4	**scallions,** chopped
$^1/_2$–I cup	**instant potatoes**
$^1/_4$ cup	**crushed peanuts**

In a large soup pot, combine all ingredients except potatoes and peanuts. Cook and stir over medium heat until blended and starting to bubble, about 10 minutes. Gradually add the potatoes to desired thickness, stirring continuously so potatoes don't stick to the pot or form lumps. Top individual servings with peanuts. Makes 3–4 servings.

PEANUT AND APPLE SOUP

2 tablespoons	**butter or margarine**
3	**medium Granny Smith apples,** peeled, cored, and diced
2	**stalks celery,** finely chopped
1/2	**small onion,** finely chopped
2 tablespoons	**flour**
4 cups	**chicken broth**
1 cup	**water**
1 cup	**peanut butter**
1/4 cup	**heavy cream**
1 teaspoon	**thyme**
2 tablespoons	**brown sugar**
	salt and pepper, to taste

In a large soup pot melt butter and add the apples, celery, and onion. Cook and stir on medium heat until celery and onion are translucent, about 10 minutes. Add the flour and continue cooking 2 minutes, stirring continuously. Add broth, water, and peanut butter. Bring to a slow boil, allowing to bubble for about 3 minutes on medium-high heat, stirring to prevent sticking. Reduce heat to low, cover, and continue to cook for 15 minutes, stirring occasionally. Add cream, thyme, sugar, salt, and pepper; stir until well blended and continue to cook 3 more minutes. Makes 3–4 servings.

JELLED STRAWBERRY AND PEANUT SALAD

I small box (3.4 ounces)	**strawberry gelatin**
I cup	**boiling water**
I package (10 ounces)	**frozen sliced strawberries**
I can (8 ounces)	**crushed pineapple,** drained
2	**bananas,** peeled and sliced
I cup	**chopped peanuts**
$\frac{1}{2}$ cup	**peanut butter**
I cup	**sour cream**
2 teaspoons	**brown sugar**

Combine gelatin and water in a medium saucepan over high heat. Stir until dissolved and water starts to boil. Add strawberries, pineapple, bananas, and peanuts. Mix well and remove from heat. Pour into a 9 x 9-inch dish and refrigerate until firm, about 2 hours.

In a small bowl, combine peanut butter, sour cream, and sugar. Mix well and spread over top of salad when set and ready to serve. Makes 6 servings.

CONFETTI FREEZER SALAD

¹/₄ cup	**peanut butter**
3 ounces	**cream cheese,** softened
¹/₃ cup	**mayonnaise**
I teaspoon	**lemon juice**
2	**egg whites**
¹/₃ cup	**sugar**
I cup	**whipped cream**
I cup	**small marshmallows**
¹/₄ cup	**Mandarin oranges**
I can (I5 ounces)	**fruit cocktail,** drained
¹/₂ cup	**maraschino cherries**

In a large bowl, mix the peanut butter, cream cheese, mayonnaise, and lemon juice together until well combined.

In a small bowl, beat the egg whites with a hand mixer until foamy. Add the sugar in increments and continue beating until stiff peaks form. Fold the whipped cream into the stiffened egg whites. Fold the egg whites into the peanut butter mixture and add the marshmallows and fruit. Pour mixture into an 8 x 8-inch dish and freeze until firm. Makes 6–8 servings.

ZESTY SHRIMP SALAD

1 pound	**large shrimp,** peeled and deveined
1 bag (10.5 ounces)	**mixed salad greens**
1/4 cup	**chopped red onion**
1/2	**small red or yellow bell pepper,** seeded and chopped
2	**eggs,** boiled, peeled, and chopped
1	**lemon, juice and zest**
1/3 cup	**peanut butter**
2 tablespoons	**red pepper flakes**
1 tablespoon	**brown sugar**
1 cup	**croutons**

Place shrimp in a large saucepan with enough water to cover, and cook until water boils and shrimp start to turn pink. Do not overcook. Remove shrimp from boiling water and place in a cold water bath to stop cooking. Drain and place in a medium bowl; set aside.

Combine salad greens in a large bowl with the onion, bell pepper, and eggs.

In a small bowl combine the lemon juice, zest, peanut butter, pepper flakes, and sugar, mix well. If too thick, add a few drops of water to desired consistency. Pour dressing over the shrimp and toss to coat.

Add shrimp to salad greens and top with croutons. Serve immediately. Makes 3–4 Servings.

PARADISE PEANUT SLAW

1	**medium head red cabbage,** chopped
1	**medium bok choy cabbage,** chopped
1	**cup grated carrots**
1/2 cup	**chopped celery**
1 cup	**grated jicama**
1/3 cup	**dried cranberries**
1/3 cup	**chopped dried pineapple**
1/3 cup	**crunchy peanut butter**
1/3 cup	**plain yogurt**
1/3 cup	**Asian salad dressing**
1/2 cup	**peanuts**

In a large bowl, add the cabbages, carrots, celery, jicama, cranberries, and pineapple. Toss to mix.

Blend the peanut butter, yogurt, and dressing together in a small bowl and mix well. Pour over salad and toss to coat. Sprinkle peanuts over top before serving. Makes 6 servings.

ZIPPY POTATO SALAD

8	**medium Yukon Gold potatoes**
3–4	**chopped green onions**
1/3 cup	**chopped cilantro or parsley**
1/3 cup	**chopped celery**
1/3 cup	**chopped peanuts**
1/2 container (3 ounces)	**plain yogurt**
3–4 teaspoons	**Miracle Whip**
1/2 cup	**crunchy peanut butter**
1 teaspoon	**paprika**
	salt and pepper, to taste

Scrub and wash potatoes; you can either peel or leave the skins on. Cut into quarters and place in a large saucepan with enough water to cover. Boil in salted water for 15 minutes, or until tender. Drain water and place potatoes in a medium bowl. Add the onions, cilantro, celery, and peanuts. Toss to mix.

Combine the yogurt, Miracle Whip, peanut butter, paprika, salt, and pepper in a blender and pulse until creamy. Add to potatoes and toss to coat. Serve warm or cold. Makes 6 servings.

SOUTHERN SWEET POTATOES

¼ cup	**butter or margarine**
2 cans (29 ounces each)	**sweet potatoes or yams in syrup,** liquid reserved
¾ cup	**crunchy peanut butter**
½ cup	**brown sugar**
¼ cup	**pineapple juice**
4 tablespoons	**vanilla extract**
3 teaspoons	**maraschino cherry juice**
1½ cups	**chopped pecans**
3–4 cups	**miniature marshmallows**

Preheat oven to 350 degrees.

Melt the butter in a 9 x 13-inch baking dish. Cut the sweet potatoes into uniform pieces and place in the dish.

In a small bowl, combine the peanut butter, sugar, pineapple juice, vanilla, cherry juice, and ½ cup of the reserved liquid. Pour mixture over potatoes. Sprinkle pecans on top and completely cover with the marshmallows. Bake for 15–20 minutes, or until the marshmallows start to brown. Makes 6 servings.

PEANUT BUTTER POTATO CAKES

2 cups	**mashed potatoes**
1/3 cup	**peanut butter**
1	**egg**
2 tablespoons	**flour**
1	**green onion,** chopped
1/2 teaspoon	**red pepper flakes**
	salt, to taste
	milk, for desired consistency
3 tablespoons	**peanut oil**

In a large bowl, mix all the ingredients together except oil. You can control how thick or dry the mixture will be by adding the milk a little bit at a time.

Add oil to a large frying pan and heat to medium-high. Oil will be ready for frying when a drop of water pops up from the pan.

Divide potato mixture into 8 equal portions and form into patties. Add to pan and cook on each side 4–5 minutes, turning once. Remove cooked patties to a warm plate and cover with paper towels until ready to serve. Makes 8 servings.

PEANUT BUTTER BISCUITS

2 cups	**sifted flour**
2 tablespoons	**baking powder**
$1/2$ teaspoon	**baking soda**
$1/3$ cup	**peanut butter**
$1/4$ cup	**shortening**
$3/4$ cup	**buttermilk**

Preheat oven to 450 degrees.

Place all ingredients in a large bowl and mix until well combined. Knead gently and roll dough out on a floured surface to $1/2$-inch thick. Use a biscuit cutter to cut biscuits. Place on a baking sheet prepared with nonstick cooking spray and bake for 10–15 minutes, or until golden brown. Makes 12.

VEGAN
LOVERS

VEGAN "SALMON" PARTY SPREAD

6 ounces	**smoked tofu***
I can (16 ounces)	**garbanzo beans,** drained and rinsed
4 tablespoons	**peanut butter**
I tablespoon	**tahini**
I tablespoon	**lime juice**
½ teaspoon	**Liquid Smoke**
	soy or rice milk
2 tablespoons	**chopped fresh parsley**

Place all ingredients except parsley into bowl of a food processor and pulse until it reaches a spreadable consistency, adding milk as needed to desired consistency. Remove from bowl and shape into a loaf. Garnish with parsley. Makes 1 ½ cups.

Serve with fresh vegetables of choice and crackers. Refrigerate leftovers.

*NOTE: Found packaged alongside extra-firm or regular tofu at most full service grocers such as Whole Foods, Winco, Trader Joe's, and Asian grocers. If unavailable, buy regular silken and add 1–2 drops of Liquid Smoke, but not more than 2 drops.

ROASTED PEANUT AND GARLIC AIOLI

4	**garlic bulbs,** husks removed
1/4 cup	**olive oil**
1/2 cup	**Vegenaise or other vegan mayonnaise**
1 tablespoon	**Dijon mustard**
1 tablespoon	**lemon juice**
1/4 cup	**finely chopped roasted peanuts**
4 tablespoons	**peanut butter**
2 tablespoons	**chives**

Preheat oven to 400 degrees.

Place garlic on a baking sheet and drizzle oil over tops. Bake uncovered for 20 minutes, or until soft.

When garlic has finished roasting, separate the cloves and squeeze out the softened garlic into a small bowl. Add the mayonnaise, mustard, lemon juice, peanuts, peanut butter, and chives. Mix until well combined. Keep refrigerated until ready to serve. Makes 1 cup.

Serve with crackers, rustic breads, drizzled over grilled or steamed veggies or roasted potatoes.

BREAKFAST SCRAMBLE

1 package (14 ounces)	**extra-firm tofu**
2 tablespoons	**vegetable oil**
1 tablespoon	**crushed garlic**
1 teaspoon	**onion powder**
4 tablespoons	**crunchy peanut butter**
1/2 cup	**nutritional yeast**
1/2 cup	**chopped fresh mushrooms**
1	**scallion,** sliced
1/2	**small green bell pepper,** seeded and chopped

Drain and crumble the tofu into small pieces. In a medium frying pan, saute tofu in oil for 5 minutes. Add remaining ingredients and stir-fry until vegetables have softened, about 4 minutes. Serve warm. Makes 3 servings.

CRUNCHY EGGPLANT

4	**long, thin eggplants**
6 tablespoons	**peanut butter**
3 teaspoons	**vinegar**
2 teaspoons	**sesame oil**
1 tablespoon	**sugar**
2 teaspoons	**chopped fresh ginger**
3 tablespoons	**water**
1 teaspoon	**hot chili sauce**
1/8 cup	**sesame seeds**
1 1/2 cups	**French's French Fried Onions**
1/4 cup	**chopped cilantro or parsley**

Preheat oven to 400 degrees.

Scrub eggplant under cold water, dry, and cut into long, thin slices. Place slices in a large microwave safe container, cover with water, and cook in microwave on high until soft, about 10 minutes.

In a small bowl, combine peanut butter, vinegar, oil, sugar, ginger, water, and chili sauce. Whisk until smooth.

Remove eggplant from microwave, drain water, and place on a baking sheet that has been prepared with vegan butter or nonstick cooking spray. Pour sauce over the eggplant and sprinkle sesame seeds and onions over top. Bake for 10 minutes, or until crunchy. Garnish with cilantro before serving. Makes 4 servings.

PEANUT BUTTER PUMPKIN SOUP

1	**medium pumpkin,** (approximately 10 pounds)
2 cans (16 ounces each)	**kidney beans,** drained and rinsed
1	**small green bell pepper,** seeded and chopped
1	**small onion,** peeled and chopped
6–8	**medium potatoes,** diced
4–5	**medium carrots,** peeled and sliced
1 can (15 ounces)	**cream-style corn**
2	**garlic cloves,** peeled and mashed
4 cups	**vegetable stock**
1 cup	**peanut butter**
1 can (10 ounces)	**Rotel Chunky Tomatoes & Green Chilies**
1 teaspoon	**ground sage**
1 teaspoon	**ground cumin**
	salt and pepper, to taste

Preheat oven to 350 degrees.

Carve out top of pumpkin. Clean the pumpkin by removing the stringy pulp and seeds. Cut interior pumpkin meat into cubes and remove. Be careful not to cut too deep. The shell needs to be sturdy enough to hold up during the baking time.

In a large soup pot, simmer pumpkin cubes and remaining ingredients for 40 minutes, stirring occasionally to prevent sticking. Place the empty pumpkin in a shallow roasting pan and add the soup to the pumpkin. Bake uncovered for 2 hours, or until the pumpkin exterior becomes tender, but not collapsed, checking every 30 minutes. Makes 6 servings.

VEGAN GUMBO

3 tablespoons	**olive oil,** divided
I package (12 ounces)	**frozen sliced okra**
I package (16 ounces)	**vegan sausage links,** cut into pieces
3 tablespoons	**flour**
I	**large onion,** peeled and chopped
I	**medium red bell pepper,** seeded and chopped
$^1/_2$ cup	**crunchy peanut butter**
2 teaspoons	**red pepper flakes**
I tablespoon	**Creole seasoning**
3	**garlic cloves,** peeled and mashed
I can (16 ounces)	**diced tomatoes,** with liquid
2	**stalks celery,** chopped
5 cups	**vegetable stock**
I package (12 ounces)	**frozen lima beans**
2 tablespoons	**Tabasco Sauce**
	salt and pepper, to taste
$2^1/_2$ cups	**cooked rice**

In a large frying pan, heat 2 tablespoons of oil on medium-high heat. Add the okra and sausage and cook for 8–10 minutes, or until sausage is heated through. Remove from pan and set aside.

In same frying pan, combine flour and remaining oil and saute for I minute on medium-high heat. Add the okra, sausage, onion, bell pepper, peanut butter, pepper flakes, seasoning, and garlic. Stir constantly for 2 minutes to prevent sticking. Stir in the tomatoes, celery, stock, and lima beans. Cover and cook on medium-low heat for 20–25 minutes, or until the lima beans are thoroughly cooked. Stir in Tabasco, salt, pepper, and cooked rice before serving. Makes 6 servings.

CHOWDA

I package (14 ounces)	**extra-firm tofu,** cubed
1/3 cup	**peanut butter**
4 cubes	**vegetable bouillon**
2 1/2 cups	**coconut milk**
2 cups	**water**
I container (8 ounces)	**sliced fresh mushrooms**
6–8	**green onions,** sliced
4	**large Yukon Gold or russet potatoes,** cubed
I cup	**julienned carrots**
1/2 cup	**chopped celery**
6–8	**vegan bacon strips,** chopped
I	**lime,** juiced
2 1/2 tablespoons	**soy sauce**
4	**garlic cloves,** peeled and minced

In a large soup pot over medium-high heat, add tofu, peanut butter, bouillon, milk, and water. Bring to a boil, turn down heat, and let simmer for 5 minutes. Add vegetables, bacon, lime juice, soy sauce, and garlic. Simmer on medium heat for 20 minutes, or until vegetables are tender. Makes 4 servings.

BARBECUED TOFU

1 package (14 ounces)	**extra-firm tofu**
2	**lemons, juice and zest**
1/4 cup	**orange juice**
1/2 cup	**peanut butter**
3 tablespoons	**maple syrup**
2 tablespoons	**vinegar**
2 teaspoons	**fresh rosemary**
3	**garlic cloves,** peeled and chopped
2 teaspoons	**soy sauce**
dash	**olive oil**
	pepper, to taste

Slice tofu into 8 pieces and place in a large ziplock bag. In a small bowl, whisk remaining ingredients together until well blended. Pour marinade over tofu and refrigerate for 8 hours, or overnight.

Place tofu on grill rack prepared with oil to prevent sticking and grill over medium heat for 5 minutes on each side. Serve on buns. Makes 4 servings.

MOTHER EARTH'S MEATLOAF

1 pound	**vegan ground beef**
3 tablespoons	**ketchup**
1 tablespoon	**prepared mustard**
6 tablespoons	**peanut butter**
1 tablespoon	**horseradish**
$1/2$	**small onion,** peeled and chopped
$1/2$	**small green bell pepper,** seeded and chopped
$1/2$ cup	**breadcrumbs**
$1/4$ cup	**soy or almond milk**
$1/2$ tablespoon	**soy sauce**
	salt and pepper, to taste

Preheat oven to 350 degrees.

In a large bowl, add all ingredients and mix until well combined. Shape into a loaf and place in loaf pan that has been prepared with nonstick cooking spray. Cover with foil and bake for 1 hour and 15 minutes. Makes 4 servings.

VEGAN PEANUT BUTTER BARS

²/₃ cup	**soy margarine**
1 ½ teaspoons	**vanilla extract**
½ cup	**peanut butter**
1 teaspoon	**salt**
1 cup	**sugar**
2 cups	**flour**
1 cup	**vegan chocolate chips**
1 cup	**chopped peanuts**

Preheat oven to 375 degrees.

In a small saucepan, heat margarine, vanilla, peanut butter, and salt over medium heat until melted. Stir to combine. Transfer to a large bowl, add sugar, and beat with electric mixer until fluffy. Add flour and mix to combine. Stir in chocolate chips.

Spread mixture in a 9 x 13-inch pan that has been lightly prepared with nonstick cooking spray. Sprinkle peanuts evenly over top, pressing gently into mixture. Bake for 20 minutes, or until a toothpick inserted into the center comes out clean. Cut into squares while still warm. Makes 12 bars.

ALIEN BITES

1/2 cup	**favorite vegan granola**
1/4 cup	**roasted sunflower seeds**
1/2 cup	**raisins**
1/4 cup	**grated carrots**
3–4 tablespoons	**brown sugar**
1/4 cup	**crystallized ginger pieces**
1 cup	**peanut butter**
1 cup	**vegan chocolate chips**

In a medium bowl, mix all ingredients together except peanut butter and chocolate chips. Blend in peanut butter a few spoonfuls at a time, stirring until well combined. Cover and refrigerate overnight.

Place chocolate chips in a small microwave safe bowl and microwave for 1 1/2–2 minutes on high, stirring every 20 seconds until smooth.

Form mixture into 1-inch balls and dip into melted chocolate, covering completely. Place on a baking sheet that has been covered with parchment or wax paper and refrigerate for at least 1 hour before serving. Makes 2 dozen.

FAUX MOO PIE

1 package (12 ounces)	**vegan chocolate chips**
1 package (14 ounces)	**firm tofu**
1 1/2 cups	**peanut butter**
1/4 cup	**soy or almond milk**
1 cup	**chopped nuts of choice**
1 (9-inch)	**graham cracker pie crust**

In a small microwave safe bowl, melt chocolate chips in microwave for 1 1/2–2 minutes on high, stirring every 20 seconds until smooth.

In a food processor or blender, add the melted chocolate, tofu, peanut butter, and milk. Blend until smooth. Add the nuts and stir by hand until well combined. Pour mixture into pie crust and refrigerate for 2–3 hours. Makes 6–8 servings.

If you desire a hard topping, melt 1 cup of vegan chocolate chips and pour over top of chilled pie. Refrigerate again for 2–3 more hours.

SWEET
TREATS

PERFECT PEANUT BUTTER FROSTING

2 cups	**powdered sugar**
1/3 cup	**peanut butter**
2 teaspoons	**butter or margarine**
3–5 teaspoons	**milk**
1 teaspoon	**vanilla extract**

Combine all ingredients in a medium bowl and beat with a hand mixer until smooth, adding milk in increments to desired consistency. Frosting should be thick. Makes 2 cups.

NO STIR-CRAZY COOKIE BARS

¼ cup	**butter or margarine,** melted
2 cups	**graham cracker crumbs**
1 bag (7 ounces)	**shredded coconut**
1 package (6 ounces)	**butterscotch chips**
1 package (6 ounces)	**peanut butter chips**
1 can (14 ounces)	**sweetened condensed milk**
1 cup	**chopped pecans**

Preheat oven to 325 degrees.

Pour melted butter into a 9 x 9-inch pan and add ingredients by even layers in the order listed. Do not stir. Bake for 20 minutes. Allow to cool in pan before cutting into squares. Makes 12–16 bars.

LAZY DAY BARS

2 cups	**graham cracker crumbs**
2 cups	**powdered sugar**
1 ⅛ cups	**peanut butter,** divided
½ cup	**butter or margarine,** melted
1 ½ cups	**milk chocolate chips**

In a large bowl, mix together the cracker crumbs, sugar, 1 cup peanut butter, and butter until well combined. Press mixture into the bottom of a 9 x 9-inch pan.

In a medium microwave safe bowl, melt the chocolate chips and remaining peanut butter in microwave for 1 ½–2 minutes on high, stirring every 20 seconds until smooth. Pour and spread mixture over the crust. Refrigerate at least 1 hour before cutting into bars. Makes 12–16 bars.

COUNTRY CLUB BARS

1 cup	**flour**
1 teaspoon	**baking powder**
1 teaspoon	**cinnamon**
dash	**salt**
1 cup	**brown sugar**
1/2 cup	**butter or margarine**
1/2 cup	**peanut butter**
3 tablespoons	**corn syrup**
2 teaspoons	**vanilla extract**
1	**egg**

Frosting:

1 cup	**powdered sugar**
3 tablespoons	**peanut butter**
3 tablespoons	**butter or margarine,** softened
2–3 tablespoons	**milk**

Preheat oven to 350 degrees.

In a small bowl, combine the flour, baking powder, cinnamon, and salt. Stir and set aside.

In a large bowl, cream together the sugar, butter, peanut butter, and corn syrup. Add the vanilla and egg. Mix well. Gradually add in the flour mixture until well combined. Pour into an 8 x 8-inch pan that has been prepared with nonstick cooking spray. Bake for 15 minutes, or until golden brown. Allow to cool before frosting. Makes 12–18 bars.

In a small bowl, mix together the frosting ingredients, adding milk 1 tablespoon at a time to desired consistency.

BLONDIES

1/2 cup	**peanut butter**
1/2 cup	**butter or margarine,** softened
1 cup	**brown sugar**
2	**eggs**
2 teaspoons	**vanilla extract**
1 cup	**flour**
1 teaspoon	**baking powder**
1/2–1 teaspoon	**salt**
1/2 cup	**butterscotch chips**
1/2 cup	**chopped salted peanuts**

Preheat oven to 350 degrees.

Line a 9 x 9-inch pan with nonstick foil, extending beyond edges of the pan. Set aside.

In a large bowl combine the peanut butter, butter, and sugar. Mix on medium speed with electric mixer until light and fluffy. Add the eggs one at a time, mixing after each addition. Add the vanilla and continue to mix until well combined.

In a small bowl, mix together the flour, baking powder, and salt. Slowly add flour mixture to peanut butter mixture on low speed and blend well. Stir in butterscotch chips and peanuts. Pour batter into pan and bake for 20 minutes. When cool, lift out by using the extended foil and then cut into bars. Makes 12 bars.

PEANUT BUTTER AND JELLY BARS

1 cup	**butter or margarine**
1 ½ cups	**sugar**
2 ½ cups	**peanut butter**
2	**eggs**
2 teaspoons	**vanilla extract**
3 cups	**flour**
1 teaspoon	**baking powder**
2 teaspoons	**salt**
2 cups	**jam,** of choice

Preheat oven to 350 degrees.

In a large bowl, beat together the butter and sugar with an electric mixer for about 2 minutes. Add the peanut butter, eggs, and vanilla and beat 2 minutes more.

In a medium bowl, combine the flour, baking powder, and salt. Add flour to peanut butter mixture in increments, using a low speed until well combined.

Pour a little more than half of the batter into a 9 x 13-inch pan that has been prepared with nonstick cooking spray. Spread the jam over this mixture and spoon the remaining batter on top of the jam. Bake for 35–40 minutes. Allow to cool and cut into bars. Makes 24–30 bars.

PEANUT BUTTER COOKIES

1 can (14 ounces)	**sweetened condensed milk**
¾ cup	**peanut butter**
2 cups	**biscuit mix**
1 teaspoon	**vanilla extract**
⅓ cup	**sugar**

Preheat oven to 375 degrees.

In a large bowl, mix milk and peanut butter together until smooth. Add biscuit mix and vanilla and mix well. Shape dough into 1-inch balls and roll in the sugar.

Flatten dough balls slightly by hand and place 2 inches apart on an ungreased baking sheet. Bake for 6–8 minutes. Makes 24.

FLAT TIRES

1 cup	**butter or margarine**
1/4 cup	**peanut butter**
1 cup	**sugar**
1	**egg yolk**
2 cups	**flour**
1 teaspoon	**cinnamon**
1 teaspoon	**vanilla extract**

Frosting:

1/3 cup	**peanut butter**
3 cups	**powdered sugar**
1/4 cup	**milk**
2 teaspoons	**vanilla extract**
1/4 cup	**butter or margarine**

Preheat oven to 375 degrees.

In a large bowl, mix butter, peanut butter, sugar, egg yolk, flour, cinnamon, and vanilla together until well combined. Spread batter in a 9 x 13-inch baking sheet that has been lightly prepared with nonstick cooking spray. Bake for 8–12 minutes.

In a large bowl, mix together frosting ingredients until smooth and pour over cookies while still hot. Allow to cool slightly and cut into portions. Makes 12.

PEANUT BUTTER CAKE BALLS

1 box (15.25 ounces)	**cake mix,** of choice
1 can (16 ounces)	**prepared frosting,** of choice
1 bag (12 ounces)	**peanut butter chips**
1 bar (8 ounces)	**almond bark**
12 or more	**Andes Mints**

Prepare and bake cake per box instructions. Remove from oven and cool slightly.

In a large bowl, break warm cake into pieces and add half of the can of frosting, or as desired. The warmer the cake, the less frosting you'll need. Add the peanut butter chips. Mix and crumble ingredients together.

Shape mixture into 1-inch balls. Place on baking sheet that has been covered with parchment or waxed paper, and then place in freezer for approximately 2 hours.

In a medium microwave safe bowl, melt the almond bark and mints for 1 1/2–2 minutes on high, stirring every 20 seconds until very smooth to create the icing. Remove cake balls from freezer and dip them one at a time into the prepared icing. Place back on waxed paper to harden before serving. Makes 24.

PEANUT BUTTER PARTY CUPS

1 package (16.5 ounces) **refrigerated peanut butter cookie dough**
ice cream, fruit, nuts, candies, or pudding, of choice

Preheat oven to 325 degrees.

Prepare a 12-cup muffin pan with nonstick cooking spray.

Press 2 squares of dough into the bottom and up the sides of each muffin cup. Bake for 12–15 minutes, or until golden. After cooling, remove from muffin pan. If the middle of each cup isn't deep enough, remove some of the cooked dough and discard. Serve with your choice of fillings. Makes 12 servings.

MOVIE NIGHT GRAB BAG

1 cup	**peanut butter**
1 package (12 ounces)	**peanut butter chips**
1/2 cup	**butter or margarine**
1 box (13 ounces)	**Chex cereal,** of choice
2 cups	**roasted peanuts**
2 cups	**M&M candies,** of choice
4	**paper lunch bags**
1/2 cup	**powdered sugar**

In a medium saucepan, heat peanut butter, chips, and butter over medium heat until melted. Stir until well combined.

Place cereal in a large, deep bowl and pour melted peanut butter mixture over top, stirring until thoroughly coated. After well incorporated, mix in the peanuts and let cool for a few minutes before adding M&M's to prevent melting candies.

Divide cereal mix evenly into the lunch bags, sprinkle powdered sugar into each bag, and shake until coated. Makes 4 servings.

PEANUT BUTTER AND CHOCOLATE EGGS

6–7 tablespoons	**peanut butter**
1 cup	**powdered sugar**
5 tablespoons	**butter or margarine,** softened
1 teaspoon	**vanilla extract**
1 teaspoon	**milk**
1 package (6 ounces)	**milk chocolate, semi-sweet, or white chocolate chips**

In a medium bowl, mix all ingredients together except chocolate chips. Divide mixture in 12 equal portions and roll each portion by hand into an egg shape. If necessary, add more milk a drop or two at a time to achieve desired consistency.

Place chips in a medium microwave safe bowl and microwave for 1 1/2–2 minutes on high, stirring every 20 seconds until smooth. Using a large spoon, dip each egg into the melted chocolate and completely cover. Allow to harden on waxed or parchment paper. Makes 12.

NEEDLE-IN-A-HAYSTACK

2 bags	**popped microwave popcorn,** of choice
2 cups	**crunchy chow mein noodles**
2 cups	**dry roasted peanuts**
I cup	**shredded coconut**
2 cups	**chopped pretzel sticks**
I bag (12 ounces)	**peanut butter chips**

In a large bowl, combine popcorn, noodles, peanuts, coconut, and pretzels.

Place peanut butter chips in a medium microwave safe bowl and microwave for I 1/2–2 minutes on high, stirring every 20 seconds until melted. Pour melted chips over popcorn mix, stirring to coat. Drop by spoonfuls onto waxed paper. Refrigerate to set up before serving. Makes 2 dozen.

PORCUPINES

1 cup	**peanut butter**
3 tablespoons	**butter or margarine,** softened
⅔ cup	**powdered sugar**
1 cup	**brown sugar,** divided
½ bag (14–16 ounces)	**large twist pretzels**
1 bag (12 ounces)	**milk chocolate chips**
½ bag (14–16 ounces)	**thin pretzel sticks**

In a medium bowl, combine peanut butter and butter, incorporating until well blended. Add powdered sugar and ¾ cup brown sugar; mix well.

Form mixture into golf ball-size balls. If these are not rolling easily, then add more of the brown sugar. Place each ball on a pretzel, using pretzel as a base. Place on a baking sheet prepared with wax or parchment paper and put in the freezer for 30–40 minutes.

Place chocolate chips in a medium microwave safe bowl and microwave for 1 ½-2 minutes on high, stirring every 20 seconds until melted. Dip pretzel sticks one at a time into the melted chocolate, covering only half of the stick.

Remove porcupine bodies from the freezer and poke several pretzel sticks into each body so they stick chocolate side out, resembling quills. If you're creative and have the time, make faces for your porcupines using assorted candies and cake decorating tools. Return to freezer until ready to serve. Makes 15–20.

PEANUT BUTTER
SESAME DROPS

¾ cup	**peanut butter**
½ cup	**honey**
I teaspoon	**vanilla extract**
¾ cup	**powdered milk**
I cup	**oatmeal**
¼ cup	**toasted sesame seeds**
2 tablespoons	**hot water**
I cup	**crushed nuts,** of choice

In a medium bowl, combine peanut butter, honey, and vanilla.
Mix well.

In a small bowl, mix together the powdered milk and oatmeal. Add this
mixture to the peanut butter, blending well. Stir in sesame seeds and
water. Form into 1-inch balls and roll in nuts to coat. Place on a baking
sheet lined with waxed paper until ready to serve. Makes 24.

LITTLE DARLIN'S TRAIL MIX

2 boxes (4.3 ounces each)	**animal crackers**
1 cup	**salted peanuts**
2 cups	**Reese's Pieces candies**
2 cups	**roasted sunflower seeds**
1 1/2 cups	**yogurt covered raisins**

Mix all ingredients together in a large bowl and divide equally into 4 treat bags. Makes 4 servings.

DESSERTS

MEMPHIS DECADENCE

I large box (5 ounces)	**instant vanilla pudding mix**
2 cups	**milk**
I can (14 ounces)	**sweetened condensed milk**
I cup	**peanut butter**
3 teaspoons	**vanilla extract,** divided
4	**egg whites**
1/4 teaspoon	**cream of tartar**
1/2 cup	**sugar**
I	**angel food cake or sponge cake,** cut into I-inch cubes
6	**bananas,** peeled and sliced
I cup	**crushed honey roasted peanuts**

Preheat oven to 325 degrees.

In a large bowl, add pudding mix and milk. Beat with electric mixer on medium speed for 2 minutes. Set aside.

In a medium bowl add the condensed milk, peanut butter, and 2 teaspoons vanilla. Beat until very smooth. Add to the pudding and mix until well combined.

In a large bowl, beat egg whites with cream of tartar and I teaspoon vanilla until peaks begin to form. Add the sugar in increments, beating after each addition. Continue beating until stiff peaks have formed.

To assemble, create layers in a deep 10-inch oven-safe glass bowl beginning with cake cubes, pudding, bananas, and meringue. Repeat layers, sprinkling peanuts over top layer. Bake for 10 minutes, or until the meringue peaks begin to brown very lightly. Makes 8 servings.

PEANUT BUTTER BREAD PUDDING

1 ½ cups	**milk**
1 cup	**sugar**
4	**eggs**
3 slices	**bread,** torn into small pieces
½ cup	**peanut butter**
2 teaspoons	**vanilla extract**
½ cup	**raisins**
1 tablespoon	**butter or margarine**
1 teaspoon	**cinnamon**

Sauce:

½ cup	**sugar**
1 tablespoon	**flour**
1 cup	**milk**
2 teaspoons	**vanilla extract**

Preheat oven to 350 degrees.

In a large saucepan, heat milk until it just starts to steam. Beat the sugar and eggs together and add to the milk. Stir quickly for about 10 seconds, and remove from stove.

Add the bread, peanut butter, vanilla, and raisins to milk mixture. Stir well to combine and pour into an 8 x 8-inch pan that has been prepared with nonstick cooking spray. Dab the butter on top, and sprinkle with cinnamon. Bake for 45 minutes. Makes 6 servings.

Add sauce ingredients to a small saucepan and cook and stir over medium heat for about 2 minutes, or until it starts to thicken. Pour sauce over warm bread pudding before serving.

PEANUT BUTTER FLAN

1 1/4 cups	**sugar,** divided
2 cups	**milk**
2 cups	**half-and-half**
6	**eggs**
1/4 cup	**peanut butter**
2 teaspoons	**vanilla extract**
dash	**salt**

Preheat oven to 325 degrees.

In a small saucepan, add 3/4 cup of sugar, cooking and stirring over medium heat until sugar turns to a light brown syrup. Remove from heat and pour into a flan pan or shallow glass pie dish. Tilt and cover bottom and sides of pan evenly with syrup and set aside.

In a large saucepan, heat milk and half-and-half until bubbles form around edges. Remove from heat. In a large bowl, beat eggs, adding peanut butter, remaining sugar, vanilla, and salt until well combined. Gradually stir hot milk into egg mixture, blending together well. Pour in dish prepared with syrup.

Set dish in a larger shallow pan and pour up to a 1/2 inch of boiling water into bottom of pan. Bake for 35–40 minutes, or until a butter knife inserted between the center and the edge comes out clean. Allow flan to cool before placing in refrigerator for at least 4 hours, or overnight. To serve, loosen flan by running a wet knife around edges, shaking gently to release, and invert onto a plate. Makes 6–8 servings.

DESSERT PIZZA

1 container (16.5 ounces)	**refrigerated peanut butter cookie dough**
1/2 cup	**peanut butter**
4 ounces	**cream cheese,** softened
1/2 cup	**powdered sugar**
1 container (8 ounces)	**frozen whipped topping,** thawed
3 cups	**assorted fresh fruit; strawberries, blueberries, kiwi, raspberries, bananas, pineapple, or coconut**
1 cup	**crushed hard candies,** of choice

Preheat oven to 350 degrees.

Press cookie dough into a 10-inch pizza pan and bake for 12–18 minutes, or until golden brown. Set aside and let cool.

In a medium bowl, mix together peanut butter, cream cheese, and sugar. Fold in whipped topping and spread over baked cookie dough. Top with fruit and crushed candies. Makes 4 servings.

PEAR AND PEANUT BUTTER CRISP

2 cans (16 ounces each)	**pear halves,** drained, liquid reserved
3–4 tablespoons	**crystallized ginger**

Topping:

1/2 cup	**peanut butter**
2/3 cup	**rolled oats**
1/3 cup	**brown sugar**
1/4 cup	**flour**
1/2 teaspoon	**ground ginger**
1/4 cup	**butter or margarine,** cut into pieces

Preheat oven to 400 degrees.

Place drained pear halves in a 1 1/2-quart baking dish. Sprinkle ginger over top.

Add peanut butter, oats, sugar, flour, and ginger to bowl of food processor and pulse to combine. Add the butter and continue to pulse until coarse crumbs form. Spread crumbs evenly over the pears. If you prefer a crisp that isn't as dry and crunchy, you can add some of the reserved liquid from the pears before baking.

Bake for 20 minutes, or until bubbly and crumbs start to brown. Makes 4 servings.

PEANUT BUTTER TRIFLE

I box (18.5 ounces)	**brownie mix**
I large box (5 ounces)	**instant chocolate pudding**
I bag (8 ounces)	**peanut butter cups,** rough chopped
2 cups	**heavy cream**
4 tablespoons	**sugar**
I cup	**peanut butter**
8 ounces	**cream cheese,** softened
I cup	**powdered sugar**
3 tablespoons	**milk**
$1/4$-$1/3$ cup	**cocoa powder**

Prepare brownies according to package directions. Cool and cut into 1-inch cubes.

In a large bowl, prepare the pudding according to package directions. Mix in the chopped peanut butter cups. Chill and keep refrigerated until ready to use.

In a medium bowl, beat together cream and sugar with a mixer until stiff, heavy peaks form. Chill and keep refrigerated until ready to use.

In a medium bowl, mix peanut butter and cream cheese together on medium speed, scraping the blades if necessary. Add the powdered sugar and mix until well combined. Add the milk and blend well.

Begin layering in a trifle bowl starting with brownies, peanut butter mixture, pudding, and whipped cream. Repeat layers until all ingredients are used, dusting top with cocoa powder. Makes 8–10 servings.

PEANUT BUTTER AND BANANA CREAM PIE

¹/₂ cup	**white or dark chocolate flavored peanut butter**
¹/₂ cup	**chocolate chips**
3 tablespoons	**butter or margarine,** divided
1 (9-inch)	**chocolate crumb pie crust**
1 cup	**sugar**
2 tablespoons	**cornstarch**
dash	**salt**
2	**egg yolks**
2 cups	**milk**
1 teaspoon	**banana extract**
1 teaspoon	**vanilla extract**
2	**bananas,** peeled and sliced
1¹/₂ cups	**whipping cream**
2 tablespoons	**powdered sugar**

In a small saucepan over low heat, melt peanut butter, chocolate chips, and 1 tablespoon of butter. Mix well to combine and pour into pie crust; refrigerate until firm.

In a small saucepan, whisk together sugar, cornstarch, and salt. Beat egg yolks and milk together and add to sugar. Cook and stir over medium heat until mixture starts to bubble and thicken. Continue stirring for 1 minute and remove from heat. Add remaining butter, banana extract, and vanilla. Mix to combine until the butter is melted. Cool slightly. Layer banana slices in bottom of pie crust and pour warm pudding on top. Refrigerate.

In a medium bowl, beat whipping cream and powdered sugar together until stiff peaks form. Gently spread over chilled pie. Makes 6 servings.

EASY AS PIE

4 ounces	**cream cheese,** softened
³⁄₄ cup	**powdered sugar**
¹⁄₂ cup	**peanut butter**
¹⁄₂ cup	**milk**
I container (8 ounces)	**frozen whipped topping,** thawed
I (9-inch)	**shortbread pie crust**
I package (6–8 ounces)	**butterscotch chips**

In a medium bowl beat cream cheese and sugar together with a mixer until well combined. Add the peanut butter and milk and continue mixing until creamy and smooth.

Fold whipped topping into peanut butter mixture and pour into pie crust. Top with butterscotch chips and freeze for 2–3 hours before serving. Makes 6 servings.

BIRTHDAY PARTY PIE

12–16	**peanut butter sandwich cookies**
4 tablespoons	**butter or margarine,** melted
6 tablespoons	**peanut butter**
2 pints	**vanilla ice cream or favorite flavor,** softened
24	**miniature peanut butter cups**
1/2 cup	**chocolate fudge sauce**
1/3 cup	**chopped peanuts**

Place cookies in a food processor and pulse to a medium-fine crumb, or crush in a large ziplock bag with rolling pin. Place crumbs in a small bowl and add melted butter; mix to combine. Press crumbs into bottom and up sides of a 9 x 9-inch pan. Chill in freezer 15 minutes.

Stir peanut butter into the softened ice cream. Spread half of this mixture in bottom of chilled crust. Press peanut butter cups on top of filling and top with remaining ice cream. Freeze until firm, about 2 hours.

Drizzle chocolate sauce and sprinkle peanuts over top of pie before serving. Makes 6 servings.

HEATH BAR PIE

12 (0.5 ounces each)	**Heath snack-size candy bars**
1/3 cup	**crunchy peanut butter**
1 pint	**whipping cream**
2 teaspoons	**sugar**
1 teaspoon	**vanilla extract**
1 (9-inch)	**graham cracker pie crust**

Crush Heath bars in their wrappers with a hammer or rolling pin. In a medium bowl, combine crushed candy pieces and peanut butter, mixing well. Set aside.

In a large bowl using an electric mixer, whip the cream, gradually adding sugar until stiff peaks form. Fold in the vanilla. Blend the cream mixture into peanut butter mixture and pour into pie crust. Refrigerate 6 or more hours before serving. Makes 6 servings.

QUEEN OF HEARTS DESSERT

1 package (16.5 ounces)	**refrigerated peanut butter cookie dough**
6	**peanut butter granola bars,** crushed
2 bags (6 ounces each)	**chocolate chips**
1 cup	**whipping cream**
1/2 cup	**crunchy peanut butter**
1 cup	**Red Hots cinnamon candies**
1/3 cup	**chopped peanuts**

Preheat oven to 350 degrees.

Break up cookie dough into a large bowl. Knead in crushed granola bars until well combined. Press dough into bottom and up sides of a 10-inch tart pan, spring form pan, or 9 x 9-inch pan. Bake 12–15 minutes, or until light golden brown. Using back of a wooden spoon, press crust down and bake 3–5 more minutes, until darker brown. Press crust down again and allow to rest about 5 minutes.

In a medium microwave safe bowl, microwave chocolate chips and whipping cream for 1 minute on high. Stir and microwave 1 minute more, stirring every 20 seconds until chips are melted and well combined with the cream.

In a small microwave safe bowl, microwave the peanut butter for 1 minute on high. Stir peanut butter and pour into bottom of crust. Pour chocolate mixture over the peanut butter and sprinkle cinnamon candies and peanuts on top. Refrigerate 3–4 hours before serving. Makes 8 servings.

STUFFED APPLES

6	**medium Red Delicious or Fuji apples**
I cup	**crunchy peanut butter**
I teaspoon	**nutmeg**
I cup	**shredded coconut**
$^{1}/_{2}$ cup	**golden raisins**
$^{1}/_{3}$ cup	**honey**
$^{1}/_{3}$ cup	**candied orange, mango, or pineapple bits**

Preheat oven to 375 degrees.

Core apples, remove and discard center, leaving bottom of apple intact. Opening should be large enough to spoon filling easily into apples.

In a medium bowl, mix peanut butter and remaining ingredients until well combined. Divide mixture into 6 equal portions and spoon into the core of each apple. Place apples upright in a 9 x 13-inch baking pan with about 2 inches of water in bottom of pan. Bake for 35–40 minutes. Makes 6 servings.

PEANUT BUTTER CHEESECAKE

¹/₂ cup	**peanut butter**
16 ounces	**cream cheese,** softened
3	**eggs**
³/₄ cup	**sugar**
2 tablespoons	**vanilla extract**
1 (9-inch)	**graham cracker pie crust**

Topping:

1 cup	**sour cream**
¹/₄ cup	**sugar**
3 tablespoons	**peanut butter**
1 tablespoon	**vanilla extract**

Preheat oven to 350 degrees.

In a large bowl, beat the peanut butter, cream cheese, and eggs together until smooth. Add the sugar and vanilla. Mix well. Pour into graham cracker crust and bake for 30 minutes.

In a medium bowl, mix topping ingredients together until smooth and set aside. Spread the topping over the cheesecake while still warm. Turn the oven temperature to 400 degrees and return the cheesecake to the oven for 5 additional minutes. Cool completely, then refrigerate. Makes 6 servings.

PEANUT BUTTER POUND CAKE

3 cups	**sifted flour**
1 teaspoon	**baking powder**
2 teaspoons	**salt**
1/4 cup	**butter or margarine,** softened
1 cup	**peanut butter**
3 cups	**sugar**
5	**eggs**
2 teaspoons	**vanilla extract**

Frosting:

1 1/2 cups	**powdered sugar**
1/4 cup	**milk**
1/4 cup	**peanut butter**
2 tablespoons	**vanilla extract**

Preheat oven to 325 degrees. Prepare a tube or Bundt pan with nonstick cooking spray.

In a medium bowl, combine flour, baking powder, and salt; set aside.

In a large bowl, beat butter and peanut butter until smooth using electric mixer. Add sugar and continue mixing until smooth, about 4 minutes. Add the eggs, one at a time, mixing thoroughly after each addition. Stir in the vanilla and gradually add the flour to the peanut butter mixture.

Pour batter into prepared pan and bake for 1 hour and 20 minutes. Allow cake to cool.

In a medium bowl, combine frosting ingredients until smooth. Frost cake. Makes 12 servings.

PEANUT BUTTER AND APPLE ENCHILADAS

1 can (21 ounces)	**apple pie filling**
6 (8-inch)	**flour tortillas**
1 teaspoon	**cinnamon**
1/2 cup	**peanut butter**
2/3 cup	**butter or margarine**
1 cup	**sugar**
1 cup	**brown sugar**
1 cup	**water**

Preheat oven to 350 degrees.

Divide pie filling into 6 equal amounts and spoon down the center of each tortilla. Sprinkle with cinnamon. Roll up and place seam side down in a 9 x 13-inch baking pan that has been prepared with nonstick cooking spray.

In a medium saucepan, bring the peanut butter, butter, sugars, and water to boil. Simmer and stir for about 3 minutes. Pour mixture over enchiladas and let stand for 30 minutes before baking. Bake for 20 minutes. Allow to cool 10 minutes before serving. Makes 6 servings.

NOTES

NOTES

NOTES

NOTES

METRIC CONVERSION CHART

Volume Measurements		Weight Measurements		Temperature Conversion	
U.S.	**Metric**	**U.S.**	**Metric**	**Fahrenheit**	**Celsius**
1 teaspoon	5 ml	1/2 ounce	15 g	250	120
1 tablespoon	15 ml	1 ounce	30 g	300	150
1/4 cup	60 ml	3 ounces	90 g	325	160
1/3 cup	75 ml	4 ounces	115 g	350	180
1/2 cup	125 ml	8 ounces	225 g	375	190
2/3 cup	150 ml	12 ounces	350 g	400	200
3/4 cup	175 ml	1 pound	450 g	425	220
1 cup	250 ml	2 1/4 pounds	1 kg	450	230

 Check out these "101" favorites
for more tasty recipes:

Each 128 pages, $9.99

Available at bookstores or
directly from GIBBS SMITH
1.800.835.4993
www.gibbs-smith.com
101yum.com

ABOUT THE AUTHOR

Pamela Bennett grew up in Durham, North Carolina, where she graduated from Crofts College. She is the author of *Jams & Jellies in Less Than 30 Minutes* and *Peanut Butter Sweets*. She now lives in Provo, Utah.